BUSINESS NETWORKING: STRATEGIES & TIPS FOR SUCCESSFUL NETWORKING

Networking Can Be Simple
When You Know How!

Jerome Dees Jr.

INTRODUCTION

My whole life I have had a passion and yearning to help others. Growing up, I didn't know what I wanted to be, but I knew a degree in Psychology would allow me to help support the lives of those in my community. A Psychology BA, Philosophy BA and Masters In Business Administration degree later, I am putting my education and skills to work!

I have had the privilege of attending hundreds of networking events, presenting to thousands of people and seeing the lives of those around me change for the better with the development of simple skills!

The goal of this book is to help others get the most out of business networking! With us all having busy lives, each section is intended to be read in about 5 minutes. If you are networking for the first time or someone looking for new tips or tricks, there is something for everyone in this book!

SOCIAL DISTANCING

One of the things I want to discuss is the notion of **Social Distancing** and the fact that it means keeping your distance physically, not socially"! For those reading this in the future, this chapter will be a quick reminder of early 2020 and nothing more. For those of us living through COVID-19 and the uncertainty, this gives us yet another challenge to overcome when it comes to networking.

Part of networking is finding commonality with others and finding a way to meaningfully connect. Currently, most of the world has something in common which is the fact that we are sheltered in place. There are numerous ways we can virtually connect with others (discussed later), we should not use the notion that we are "socially distant" prevent us from flexing our networking muscle.

DO YOU WANT TO BE SOLD TO!?

When you go out to network, is your hope/goal to sell something to someone else? If most of us are honest, of course, we are trying to sell something! This is why we invest time and energy into attending networking events in the first place!

On the other hand, when you are out networking, do you want someone to walk up to you and sell something? It could be life insurance, their new app or many other things. If we are being honest, most of us will say "of course we don't want someone selling us something when networking!"

This was the biggest aha moment of my networking career. Realizing that I- and most others- are doing the very things we hope others won't do! Now that we know this, how can we do a better job moving forward?

There are a few tips and tricks to help you get in the right frame of mind. I will urge you to only focus on selling the idea that you are competent, potentially an expert at something and the type of person that others want to have in their network. Focus on presenting yourself in the best light and business will follow long-term.

WHAT IS YOUR GOAL FOR NETWORKING!?

As with most things, we should begin with the end in mind. This is especially true when it comes to networking. You have to have a goal for each networking experience you plan to participate in. I will tell you very honestly that I have gone to events- not had a goal- and walked away from the event before even going through the door. Networking can be uncomfortable; even for those of us who have done it hundreds of times.

As shared in the previous chapter, having a goal of "selling something", will likely come off aggressive and you will be the person that people actively avoid. I would offer that your goal should be something simple and obtainable.

Maybe your goal is to talk to 4 new people, develop one "coffee date" or even to help 3 people with something! These can be simple goals that can be accomplished without putting too much pressure on other people.

I strive to usually to help 3 people or make 2 new connections that can be mutually beneficial with each networking experience. If goals are too aggressive, you run the risk of discouraging yourself from networking which is the last thing you want to do!

HOW TO SCORE WITH NETWORKING!

One of my first workshops on networking was in partnership with SCORE in San Jose. I came up with an acronym using their organization name:

S- Social Networking Is Vital
C- Center Your Focus On the Other Person
O- Own Who You Are & Understand Your Value
R- Remember What You Hear & Act On It
E- Elevator Pitch

Social Networking is vital as people will search for you after meeting you at events. You need to make sure your content is up-to-date & relevant!

Centering your focus on the other person means actively listening, asking questions and learning how to add value (it's not about you initially!).

Owning who you are & understanding your value is important since networking is an exchange of value. Hard to do if you don't know yours....

Remembering what you hear & acting on it shows that you listened, cared and used what you obtained to support your new contact #TheGoal

Elevator Pitch is reviewed in a later chapter.

CONFIDENCE IS KEY

When you meet someone new, they will begin to form an impression of you right away. How you stand, how you talk, the way you shake their hand, eye contact, your introduction, it all matters! Networking can be a very COMPLEX process!

Within all of the above, knowing who you are and being confident in what you can do is at the center of virtually everything else contained within this book. I have an exercise I will ask you to complete regarding your value to others in a later chapter, for now, I want you to do something that may be uncomfortable. I want you to yell "I am powerful!" Did you do it?! Now do it again "I am powerful!". Ok, one more time "I am powerful!".

The trick is for you to believe what you just said! Know that there is something within you that nobody else has. You improve yourself by listening and learning from others while also having something valuable to give. If you take this mentality into all networking experiences, you will yield a much richer experience for you and those that you interact with.

YOUR INTRODUCTION IS IMPORTANT!

When we meet someone new, we often give our name and our title like that somehow fully explains every aspect of our being. "My name is Jerome and I own a consulting company" or "My name is Jerome and I am the President of Smart Selling Guru". This doesn't give people much to connect with. My approach has evolved to share my name, a few things I actually do in my role and then give my title! "My name is Jerome, I support business owners by showing them how to network and sell by adding value for others. I speak at nearly 25 conferences and workshops a year where I offer training for entrepreneurs. I am the President of Smart Selling Guru".

Introducing yourself by showing the value you have and the tasks that you actually manage will create a much clearer picture for those you interact with. If you are a student, you can say "My name is Jerome and I am fascinated by conflict management and group process which is why I am currently a student at SFSU". For those seeking work, you can use the same principles. "My name is Jerome and I provided support for Super Bowl 50, the 2019 US Open and I am currently looking for my next opportunity in the Food & Beverage space."

PRESENT/PAST/ FUTURE

When it comes to meeting new people, I have seen others mistakenly complicate networking. Our goal should be to make a connection which becomes difficult if you struggle to carry a coherent conversation. One of the techniques that has served me well is a process called **Present/Past/Future**. Here is how it works! When you meet someone new, introduce yourself and allow the other person to do the same. Once they do, ask them to tell you a little more about what they do; this is their **Present**. You can then ask the person to tell you about what they did prior; this is their **Past**. Finally, ask them what their goal for the evening is or even in life overall; this is their **Future**!

This will allow you a few different paths to success. If the person shares something that you really connect with, you can ask more questions about that topic/shared interest which is a great way to dig deeper! You will often get individuals who will turn the questions around on you! At this point, you know what's coming, have answers ready and appear more confident!

YOU DON'T LEARN MUCH WHEN YOU TALK

I know the title of this section is blunt, but I need to drive this point home so there is no confusion. When you network, you need to provide value. You provide value by listening and understanding. That is why I love Present/Past/Future as you are asking questions and listening. My experience has been that if you are talking, you aren't learning and if you don't learn, providing value is tough.

I strive to listen between 60 & 80% of the time when I meet someone new. This means I am akin to an interrogator when I first meet someone, just less aggressive with the approach. I have honestly had conversations with people where I spoke fewer than 4 sentences in 15 minutes, but by being present and listening, I created an amazing long-term relationship with someone who was a stranger at the start of the conversation.

This is not an easy thing to do! We are programmed to listen with the goal of responding or one-upping what we heard! In this case, listening and asking for more info while showing that you are paying attention is a very valuable networking skill.

HELPING IS THE BEST WAY TO NETWORK!

Think about the last person you helped with something. It could have been something small or something big, but think about that person. Were they super angry at you because you were helpful? Of course they weren't! When it comes to networking, if you are known as the person who helps others and approachable, you get way more out of the process than you can ever imagine.

The next time you go networking, introduce yourself and then ask the other person "what is something you are currently going through that you need help with". There will be people hesitant to offer an answer, but you will find some that need to share what they are going through. This level of conversation can help to create a long-lasting relationship! Think of yourself as a conduit between contacts who can helps connect people who will have value for each other. Can you imagine the world we could live in if everyone approached networking from this standpoint!?

WHERE CAN YOU FIND EVENTS?

Eventbrite- You can search for free events or paid events depending on your budget and goals.

Facebook- You can sort to networking events in your area! There are literally hundreds of events listed.

Chambers of Commerce- Chambers are an amazing source for networking events! Their whole premise is to grow relationships and connect people. Ribbon cuttings rock!!

Associations- These can be professional groups or Alumni Associations from schools you graduated from. Don't underestimate these as a source for events and connections.

Non-Profits- If you donate time or resources, these groups will sometimes bring supporters together for holiday events and appreciations.

Libraries- Great source for information and classes which include networking.

Meetup- Meetup.com allows you to specify groups you are interested in and join online which translates into real-world events.

Host Your Own Event- Put out some food, invite people to attend and create the best event out there!

DRESS THE PART

One of the things that comes up a lot at workshops I teach is the question of how we should dress when it comes to networking. The answer can be simple and complex at the same time. I personally think you should dress in a manner that is comfortable while being mindful to not overdress for the environment that you are in. Working in Silicon Valley, many mixers are populated with individuals who are simply wearing jeans and a nice shirt. Wearing suits to these can make you stand out in an uncomfortable way.

If you are in doubt when it comes to appropriate dress code, you have the option of contacting the event host and asking. You can also find pictures from past events online and see how people are dressed. It's not very likely that the team sponsoring the event will post pictures of people who are dressed in a manner contrary to what is acceptable.

There are different levels of networking events. If you are attending a local event, business casual is typically ok. If you are attending an industry-related event (at a conference or tradeshow), I'd dress like you would for a potential job interview.

ELEVATOR PITCHES DONE RIGHT

An Elevator Pitch is an approach to introducing yourself, sharing your value and asking for some sort of commitment in a condensed time period. The idea is that you are in an elevator with someone who can have a huge impact on your personal or professional career. You must find a way to communicate in 30 to 45 seconds what your value is and why they should want to know more or connect with you.

I like to take my introduction that I shared earlier and add a couple of extra lines to it. For instance:

My name is Jerome and I offer "value 1" & "value 2", I am the owner of Smart Selling Guru. I know your team (or I know you) are currently looking for xyz. My team has helped company A & B with that same opportunity and I'd love to talk with you more about helping your group. What would be the best way to connect and discuss further?

In essence, you simply want to introduce yourself through sharing things you actually do (not just your title), then give your title, review the need you know the person has and how you can support it. Finally, ask for a commitment!

WHAT IS YOUR VALUE?

Networking is about creating value for others around you. The hope is that the value you create will be reciprocated, but I have found that seeking to give has made me much happier than seeking to be fulfilled. The tricky thing about providing value is truly understanding what your value is!

At every single networking workshop I have ever conducted (over 100 at this point and counting) I will ask those in attendance what their value is. What do you do well and what is something you aren't great at. This is a question that can take a lot of self-reflection. I literally plead with people to text someone they trust and ask two simple questions:

1) What is something I am good at?
2) What is something I can do better?

You will sometimes get an answer that you don't like. Maybe a friend feels you are "flaky" or you are "never on time". By being aware of your strengths and weaknesses, you can get closer to presenting yourself in the best light through sharing your value with others at events and in life overall. **Stop reading and text a friend the two questions and see what they say!**

KEEP IT POSITIVE

We sometimes forget that people are people. We all put our pants on one leg at a time and most of us have issues in our life! While I think being honest and genuine while networking is vital, I also think that you should be careful to not overshare or go negative.

Last week I attended an event and one of the individuals had just been fired from their previous job. Wanting to be helpful, I started asking questions about what they did and what their "ideal job" might be. The conversation took a pretty negative turn regarding companies overall, their feeling on work in general and other topics that I won't share here. For all the person knew, I could have had a position open that I would now not consider them for based on the interaction.

Once again, we all have ups and downs, but you can choose rather you go to an event and how you present yourself once there. In short conversations, focus on strengths, likes, and future ambitions. If the conversation goes 20 minutes, deeper items may come up (which is ok), but the manner in which you present them matters a lot.

GO GOOGLE YOURSELF!

During workshops, I discuss how important your social networking efforts are when it comes to showcasing your value. One of the things that I think is very important is "Googling" yourself!

Do you know what comes up if someone Googles you? If not, today is the day to find out! I welcome you to Google my name "Jerome Dees Jr" and see what comes up. Do you think I would have you do this if I was concerned about what you would find?

I need you to be just as confident when it comes to someone looking you up! As you network, post things online, look to get promoted or even apply for a job, people will search for you! If you claim to be an expert on something, but you have no online footprint to substantiate that claim, that can be problematic. There are things you can do (for free) that can help improve your Google results!

- Create A Podcast
- Post Free LinkedIn Articles!
- Volunteer To Speak At Community Events
- Join Associations For Visibility
- Create A Website & Post Your Success

DON'T NETWORK SOLELY WITHIN YOUR GROUP

One of the mistakes people make when it comes to networking is simply sticking to what is comfortable. This usually means hanging out with people they already know and not venturing out to connect with new contacts. Networking- like selling- benefits from finding new people and adding to your contact pool. There are so many people in the world with experiences & skills you may not have. You will never experience these until you put yourself out there.

I highly recommend that you network with someone else to reduce some of the "scariness" that comes with networking, but you have to make a concerted effort to meet others as well. I have often found that two people walking up to two other people can be easier than one stranger walking up to another stranger.

You are more likely to gravitate towards people who are similar to you, so make the effort to seek out those who are outside of your typical circle! I've used "Networking Bingo" before which has forced me to seek out multiple people! I have a version of Networking Bingo on my website that you can download for free!

MAKE SURE YOU TEND YOUR NETWORK

We spend a lot of time trying to find new contacts when it comes to networking. The investment of preparing, attending and following-up on networking events can be high. We sometimes forget that we have a current network which should be tended too!

Do you know someone who is a teacher? Nurse or Dr? Someone in the legal profession? Even if you don't know someone directly, I would bet that someone you know does! You MUST spend time staying connected to your current networking.

How do you tend your network? The simple answer is to stay connected. It could be a couple of coffee dates per quarter or a simple text/LinkedIn message letting someone know you are thinking about them and wanted to see how things are going. Occasionally, a simple message can turn into so much more!

Start today, text that person who you used to be close to! Text that person you used to work with or those you truly appreciate in your life! I hope you will be pleasantly surprised by the responses that you get.

GETTING OUT OF AWKWARD CONVERSATIONS

You will encounter awkward people as you network. This could be inappropriate conversations, individuals who don't engage or someone trying to sell you something Here are a few tricks that I have used:

* Tell those you network with that you have a goal of talking to "x" people which you can use as an out if a conversation is not going well. "Nice talking with you, but I need to mingle a little more to hit my goal".

* Share that you are going to head to the bar or food table to grab something to eat. You can offer for them to go to, with the hope they connect with someone else along the way.

* You can use the "I have to use the restroom" reason (not my favorite), but please make sure you at least go wash your hands or something! Be truthful.

* Make sure you close the conversation. This could be "it was nice talking with you" or "I see someone I need to connect with, would you like to connect on LinkedIn".

INTROVERTS CAN NETWORK TOO!

Although I am rarely believed, I am an introvert by nature. To this day, there remains a certain level of anxiousness & nervousness regarding networking. If you can believe that networking will impact your life in a profound way, then you can find ways to overcome those feelings and thoughts that try to prevent you from doing it.

Just like going to the gym helps you develop your endurance and muscle, going out and networking will also help you develop your skill and confidence level. Take it from someone who has attended more networking events than I can count, sometimes the best thing to do is to put yourself out there and see what happens! Many of the tools and tips you encountered in this book are intended to simplify the networking process and not overcomplicate something that is already trying in itself. At the end of the day, you are one person trying to get through the day, just like others. We all have something in common if you dig deep enough.

YOU HAVE A FOUNDATION, GO BUILD A NETWORK

Please send me your networking stories as I love sharing successes at my "Take The 'Work' Out of Networking" workshops! If you are ever interested in attending a workshop or know a group or company that could use some support, I'd love to connect and see how I can add value! Thank you again for buying this book and I wish you success with your networking efforts!

www.smartselling.guru

info@smarselling.guru

Scan To Connect With Jerome On LinkedIn

ABOUT THE AUTHOR

Jerome W Dees Jr

Jerome Dees Jr grew up in West Oakland, CA. With what he saw growing up, he knew he wanted better life for his family in the future! Seeing education as a clear path to the life he wanted, Jerome obtained his Letters, Arts & Sciences Degree from Antelope Valley College, Dual Bachelors Degrees from San Francisco State University (Psychology & Philosophy of Religion) & ultimately his MBA from the University of Pheonix.

With a passion and desire to help others, Jerome started his first business at the age of 23. That business would grow into the consulting firm her operates today "Smart Selling Guru"

Viewed as an expert in catering sales and operations, Jerome has spoken at conferences across the United States to help others get the most from their programs. His true passion lies in speaking at conferences and conducting Sales & Business Networking workshops for organizations of all sizes. Jerome is married to an wonderful wife, has 4 boys and resides in San Jose, CA.

You can find more information about Jerome and Smart Selling Guru by visiting smartselling.guru.

www.ingramcontent.com/pod-product-compliance
Lightning Source LLC
Chambersburg PA
CBHW040305220526
45473CB00002B/585